PowerKiDS Readers

AMERICAN SYMBOLS
SÍMBOLOS DE AMÉRICA

THE BALD EAGLE
El ÁGUILA CALVA

Joe Gaspar

Traducción al español: Eduardo Alamán

PowerKiDS press.
New York

Published in 2014 by The Rosen Publishing Group, Inc.
29 East 21st Street, New York, NY 10010

First Edition

Editor: Amelie von Zumbusch
Book Design: Colleen Bialecki

Traducción al español: Eduardo Alamán

Photo Credits: Cover, pp. 9, 17, 19, 21, 23 iStockphoto/Thinkstock; p. 5 FloridaStock/Shutterstock.com; p. 7 Vladislav Gurfinkel/Shutterstock.com; p. 11 Natalia Lysenko/Shutterstock.com; p. 13 S. R. Maglione/ Shutterstock.com; p. 15 Takayuki Maekawa/The Image Bank/Getty Images.

Library of Congress Cataloging-in-Publication Data

Gaspar, Joe.
The bald eagle = El águila calva / by Joe Gaspar. — First Edition.
        pages cm. — (Powerkids readers. American symbols = Símbolos de América)
Includes index.
ISBN 978-1-4777-1205-4 (library binding)
1. United States—Seal—Juvenile literature. 2. Emblems, National—United States—Juvenile literature. 3. Animals— Symbolic aspects—Juvenile literature. I. Gaspar, Joe. Bald eagle. II. Gaspar, Joe. Bald eagle. Spanish. III. Title. IV. Title: Águila calva.
CD5610.G3718 2014
929.9—dc23

2012046771

Manufactured in the United States of America

CPSIA Compliance Information: Batch #S13PK4: For Further Information contact Rosen Publishing, New York, New York at 1-800-237-9932

Websites: Due to the changing nature of Internet links, PowerKids Press has developed an online list of websites related to the subject of this book. This site is updated regularly. Please use this link to access the list:
www.powerkidslinks.com/pkras/eagle/

CONTENTS

CONTENIDO

Bald eagles are big.

Las **águilas calvas** son grandes.

They are our national bird.

El águila calva es el ave nacional.

SEAL OF THE PRESIDENT OF THE UNITED STATES

E PLURIBUS UNUM

Fish is their top food.

Su alimento principal son los peces.

They live in every state but Hawaii.

Viven en todos los estados, con excepción de Hawai.

They build big nests.

Construyen grandes nidos.

Babies are called **chicks.**

Los bebés se llaman **aguiluchos.**

They see well.

Las águilas tienen muy buen sentido de la vista.

"Bald" is an old word for "white."

Se las llama "calvas" por el color blanco de las plumas de su cabeza.

Their claws are called **talons**.

Sus pies se les llaman **garras**.

Have you seen one?

¿Has visto alguna vez un águila calva?

WORDS TO KNOW!/
PALABRAS QUE DEBES SABER

bald eagle
(el) águila calva

chicks
(los) aguiluchos

talons
(las) garras